How to Make things grow

How to
Make things grow

David Wickers
and John Tuey

STUDIO VISTA London

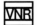 **VAN NOSTRAND REINHOLD COMPANY** New York

Acknowledgments

Drawings and diagrams are by Sharon Finmark. The authors would also like to thank Sutton and Sons Ltd, Reading, for permission to reproduce the photographs of the geranium and the hyacinth on pages 10 and 22; and Fisons Ltd, Garden Products, for permission to reproduce the photograph of re-potting on page 31 and the colour photograph of carpet bedding on page 51. The cover photographs of a daffodil appears by permission of John Waterer, Sons and Crisp Ltd.

A Studio Vista/Van Nostrand Reinhold How-to Book

Copyright © 1972 by David Wickers and John Tuey

Photoset, printed and bound in England by
BAS Printers Limited, Wallop, Hampshire

Published in Great Britain by
Studio Vista
Blue Star House, Highgate Hill, London N19
and in the United States by
Van Nostrand Reinhold Company
A Division of Litton Educational Publishing, Inc.
450 West 33rd Street, New York, N.Y. 10001

Library of Congress Catalog Card Number 76-39848

ISBN 0 289 70260 7

Contents

Introduction

In order to make things grow successfully, you should first know a few basic facts about plants. This book starts with six experiments for you to try for yourself, each of which will tell you a little more about how plants behave.

This is a book for everyone. If you live in a tall apartment block in the city you can still have gardens inside your home and display them in all manner of settings. And if you have a garden of your own, you will soon learn to apply the simple gardening techniques that will help you grow things successfully.

Everyone can have those magical 'green fingers'. You can bring colour to the dullest patch of ground, or the greenery of the countryside to your city windowsills.

Find out about plants

Experiment 1:
Plants and water
You need:

potato, knife, bowl · 2 tumblers
white carnation · potted geranium
red and blue ink · clear plastic bag, twine

1 Scrape the peel from one half of the potato and cut a slice off this end to give it a flat base.

2 Cut a hollow down into the centre of the potato at the opposite end.

3 Stand the potato in the bowl on its flat end and fill the bowl with enough water to cover the peeled area. Then watch what happens.

The water will begin to rise through tiny membranes in the potato and slowly fill the hollow in the top. This is very similar to the way in which water and minerals from the soil travel up the roots of a plant. Scientists call this process 'osmosis'.

7

1 Carefully cut along the stem of a white carnation so that the lower half divides in two.

2 Pour some red ink in one tumbler and blue in the other. Add some water to dilute the inks.

3 Stand the flower in the two glasses, with one half of the stem in the red ink and the other in the blue.

After a while, the carnation will become half red and half blue! Water is drawn up from both glasses through tiny tube-like cells in the stem to the flower itself. Even giant trees draw water from the ground up to their leaves in the same way.

The water that is drawn up from the roots and through the stem of a plant passes out into the atmosphere through minute holes in the leaves. This is called 'transpiration'.

1 Place a clear plastic bag over the potted geranium and tie it round the stem with twine so that air cannot enter.

2 Water the plant and place it in the sun.

After a few hours the inside of the bag will be coated with water. This is moisture that has been drawn up from the soil and transpired by the leaves into the air.

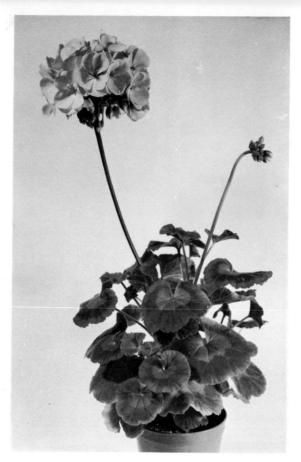

Experiment 2:
Plants and sunlight

You need:
a geranium (or other green plant), tin foil, saucer, tea-spoon, ethyl alcohol, paperclips, diluted iodine.

1 Attach a strip of tin foil to the upper surface of one of the geranium leaves with some paperclips.

2 Keep the plant in a sunny place for two to three days.

3 Remove the partly covered leaf and take off the foil. Soak it in alcohol for a few hours to take away some of the green colouring (the chlorophyll).

4 Put a few drops of iodine on the leaf with the tea-spoon and watch what happens. (Iodine is one of a number of liquids that react in one way to a substance that contains starch and in a different way to any substance that does not. Chemists can use it to find out whether or not starch is present.)

The parts of the leaf that were not covered by the foil will turn dark blue and show that starch is present. The covered part that did not get any sunlight will turn brown and show that this area lacks starch.

All green plants need sunlight in order to live. The sun supplies energy with which they make their own food or 'starch' from the carbon dioxide in air, and water. This process is called 'photosynthesis', meaning 'light to build with', and occurs because of the green 'chlorophyll' substance in the leaves.

Starch is present in many of the foods we eat. If you peel and grate some potatoes, wrap the peel in a handkerchief, and then squeeze it underwater, a powder will appear. Leave it to settle and pour away the water. When you test the powder with iodine you can prove that it is starch.

Experiment 3:
Plants and air
You need:
a green water weed
large glass jar
glass funnel
test tube
taper or long thin,
    dry stick
matches

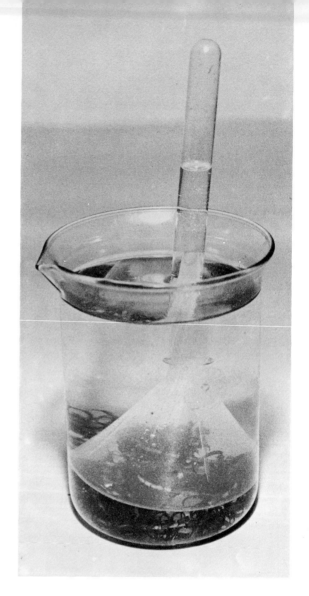

1 Fill the jar with water. Place the water plant on the bottom and cover it with the funnel.

2 Fill the test tube with water. Put your thumb over the end to avoid spilling the water and turn it upside down. Lower the end of the tube beneath the surface and fit it over the spout of the funnel.

3 Place the jar in the sunlight. Tiny bubbles of gas from the weed will gather at the top of the test tube and begin to push the water out.

4 When all the water has left the test tube, take it off the funnel, keeping your thumb over the end to prevent any gas escaping. Light the stick or taper, let it burn for a few seconds, and blow out the flame. Quickly remove your thumb from the test tube and put the end of the stick into the gas. Then watch what happens.

The stick or taper will re-light when it enters the test tube. This shows that the gas in the test tube was pure oxygen ('ordinary' air only contains about one-fifth). During photosynthesis plants produce oxygen and help to keep the balance of oxygen and carbon dioxide in the air. And so plants not only provide food for animals and humans but also oxygen for them to breathe.

Experiment 4:
Plants and movement
You need:

cotton wool	potted geranium
glass coffee jar	sawdust
bean seeds	large cardboard box
porous pot	scissors
large tin	flowerpot
potting compost	cotton
drinking straw	pin
2 thick books	white card

1 Fill the coffee jar with some wet cotton wool and slip the bean seeds between it and the sides of the jar.

2 After a few days roots will begin to grow downwards from the beans. If you turn the jar upside down and leave it for another few days, the roots will change direction and begin to grow downwards again.

Roots are attracted down towards the earth because of the force of gravity. This is known as 'geotropism'. In their search for water, however, roots do not always grow downwards.

1 Fill a large tin with sawdust and push a porous pot down into the centre. Fill the pot with water.

2 Use the bean seeds from the last experiment and plant the roots in the sawdust round the pot, leaving the beans on the surface.

After a few days, carefully brush away the sawdust around the beans and you will see that the roots have begun to grow sideways towards the water. This movement is called 'hydrotropism'.

Unlike the roots, the shoots themselves will grow towards the light they require for photosynthesis.

1 Stand a large, cardboard box upright and cut a hole in one side almost at the top. Put the potted geranium inside the box and replace the lid.

2 Stand the box in a sunny place with the hole pointing towards the sun. In a short while the geranium will begin to lean towards the hole in order to get sunlight.

3 Turn the geranium round in the box. The same thing will happen—the geranium will change position and lean towards the sunlight once more.

You have seen geotropism and hydrotropism in action—the movement of plants towards the light is called 'phototropism'.

You can also watch the rate at which plants grow, as well as the direction.

1 Soak a bean seed in water for a few hours and then plant it in a flowerpot filled with potting compost.

2 When the shoot first appears, tie one end of a short length of cotton round it. Tie the other end round the tip of a drinking straw.

3 Stand a sheet of card upright between two thick books and place the pot alongside. Pull the cotton taut and pin the straw to the card fairly near the knot, so that it points upwards.

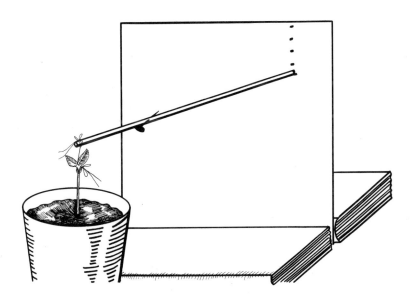

As the shoot grows, it will lift one end of the straw. The free end of the straw will move down the card. Make a mark against it at the same time each day so you can see how fast the plant is growing.

Experiment 5:
Plants and soil

You need:
screw topped jar
soil from the garden
spade
2 tin cans
2 beans

1 Half fill the jar with garden soil.

2 Fill it to the top with water, replace the cap and shake it around.

Let the jar stand. You will see that the soil separates into different layers. The heavy particles, like gravel and sand, will sink to the bottom. Next will come a layer of clay. The water itself will remain cloudy because very fine particles of clay are floating in it. On the surface you will see small, floating particles called 'humus'. This is made up of plant and animal matter which has been decayed by bacteria in the soil to make room for new plants. They provide valuable minerals on which the growing plants feed.

The soil you used is called 'topsoil' because it is found near the surface. Put some in one of the cans. Dig about 50 cm. (1½ ft.) beneath the surface and put some of this 'subsoil' in the other can. Soak two bean seeds overnight in water and plant one in each can. Keep both of them moist.

When the seedlings begin to grow, the bean planted in the topsoil will look much healthier than the one growing in the subsoil. The subsoil is less 'fertile' because it contains less humus than the topsoil.

As well as providing minerals for plants, the soil also acts as a reservoir of water for the roots, holds them in place and allows air to reach them.

Experiment 6:
Plants and reproduction
You need:
a sharp knife and a magnifying glass

Most plants produce seeds from which new plants can grow after their 'parent' plant has withered and died.

To produce fertile seeds, pollen from the stamen (the male part of the plant) has to be transferred to the pistil (the female part of the plant which contains the seeds). Soon after they have been fertilized in this way, the seeds are ready to leave the parent plant so that a few, in turn, will germinate, grow into plants, and then produce their own seeds.

Look closely at a flower and try to pick out all the different parts that perform the work of pollination. The brightly coloured petals (**a**) attract insects, such as wasps and bees, that look for nectar. These help to transfer the pollen, sometimes from the stamen to the pistil of the same plant, but usually they carry the pollen on their bodies from one plant to another. At the bottom of the pistil is the ovary (**d**). Cut this in half and you will see all the seeds inside.

Seeds may be scattered in various ways. They may be carried by the wind, like the dandelion (**e**), or the sycamore (**f**) whose seeds have wings; they may hook onto the fur of animals, like the burdock (**g**); they may float away on the surface of the water, like the water lily; they may shoot out from a pod (**h**) when it dries and splits open; and so on.

a petal	**e** dandelion
b stamens	**f** sycamore
c pistil	**g** burdock
d ovary	**h** pea

21

How to start planting and sowing

Not all plants start as seeds from flowers. Some grow from another kind of seed—the pips or stones we find inside fruit. Yet others start as bulbs or corms that look rather like onions and grow near the roots of the parent plant.

Indoor bulbs

You need:
a large bowl
bulb fibre and bulbs
   (from garden shops or chain stores)
bucket

The best time to plant bulbs is in the autumn. They will grow throughout the winter and flower in the spring. You can plant them in the garden or in a bowl indoors.

1 Put the fibre into the bucket and fill it up with water. Leave it to soak overnight.

2 Squeeze out as much water from the fibre as you can with your fingers and half fill the bowls. Do this over some old newspaper in case you make a mess.

3 Set the bulbs upright on the fibre. (The top is usually slightly pointed and the bottom is flatter, with traces of roots on it.) Arrange them in groups but not too close together or their roots will tangle (see page 23).

4 Fill up the space in between the bulbs and corms with fibre and press it down with your fingers. Leave the tops of the bulbs sticking out above the surface.

5 Place the bulb in a dark cellar or cupboard for two months. Keep the fibre moist (but do not over-water) and make sure the plants have plenty of air.

6 After two months, by which time the roots will have grown, bring the bulbs out into the light. Place them on a window sill so that they get plenty of sun, and keep the fibre moist.

You can also grow bulbs with just pebbles, charcoal and water in the bowls—or even just in water.

Bulbs and corms are really stores of food (sugar and starch) which enable the plant to grow. An onion is a bulb. If you cut one in half (**a**) with a sharp knife you will see the new flower bud surrounded by the scale leaves. When they have fed the plant they wither and turn into the brown, thin covering that surrounds the onion. A parent plant forms bulbs underground at the base of its stem.

Corms are similar to bulbs. They are a store of food for the growing plant, but when you cut one in half (**b**) you will see that it does not have scale leaves like a bulb. It is really part of the stem that grows fat with its reserves of food. A crocus is a corm (**c**).

Types of bulbs to grow
Narcissus (the daffodil is a narcissus), snowdrops, tulips.
Types of corms to grow
Crocus, gladioli, freesia.

a bulb **b** corm **c** crocus

Mustard and cress farm

You need:
thick blotting
  paper
2 saucers
mustard and
  cress seeds

1 Place a few layers of blotting paper in one saucer and soak them with water. Sprinkle the cress seeds on the paper and keep it moist.

2 A few days later do the same with the mustard seeds in the second saucer, and keep both the saucers in front of a window.

In about two weeks you will have fresh mustard and cress to put in your sandwiches.

Using the same method you can also grow the bean shoots that you eat at Chinese Restaurants. They are called 'Mung Beans' and you can buy the seeds in packets.

Sowing seeds from packets

You need:

tin trays from pies
   or frozen foods
potting compost, from a
   gardening shop
large dishes

large plastic bags
small watering can
knitting needle
variety of seeds
small corks

1 Punch some holes in the bottom of each tin tray with the knitting needle.

2 Fill each tray nearly to the top with potting compost and press down lightly. Place each tray in a dish with a cork under each corner of the tray.

3 Sprinkle a few seeds on the surface and cover them with a very thin layer of compost. Press it down lightly.

27

4 Soak the compost with water. Punch some holes in the plastic bags with the knitting needle. Place them over the seed trays and wrap them round the dishes.

5 Keep the compost moist while the seeds are growing. Take care not to let the water that comes out through the drainage holes and into the dish reach the bottom of the trays (see page 27).

When the seeds begin to sprout, place the dishes close to a window so that they get plenty of sun.

Each seed contains a tiny store of food which nourishes the plant until the roots and leaves have grown big enough to support it.

You might also like to try growing seeds in eggshells filled with potting compost and placed in the egg box.

Pips and stones

Fruit pips and stones are also seeds but because of their size it is better to grow them in small pots.

1 Soak a few pips in water overnight. (You could use orange, lemon, grapefruit, melon, cherry, grape or apple pips.)

2 Place a few stones or pieces of broken clay pot in the bottom of the flowerpots. (You could use yoghurt cartons instead, with a hole punched in the bottom.) Fill them almost to the top with potting compost.

3 Press one or two pips into each pot. Stand the pots in a saucer and keep the compost moist. Keep them away from direct sunlight until they begin to sprout.

Transplants

When the seeds have grown into seedlings, they should be replanted—either in the garden or in larger pots —to give them more room to grow.

Carefully turn one of the small pots upside down, holding the stem of the seedling lightly between the fingers of one hand, and tap the rim of the pot against the edge of a table. The plant will slide out, still firmly rooted in a ball of compost in the same way as the larger pot plant in the photograph. (If you transplant from the seed trays, carefully lift the seedlings out with the soil still around their roots using an old spoon.) Put some compost in the bottom of the larger pot, place the seedling in the middle, and fill up the rest of the space with compost (**a**). Press the surface down firmly with your fingers.

If you replant the seedlings in the garden, dig a small hole with a trowel or old spoon, pour in some water, place the ball of compost in the hole and press the soil firmly around it (**b**). Give the seedlings plenty of water at first and then keep the soil moist.

Cuttings

You can also grow some plants—roses, geraniums, chrysanthemums and apple, for example—by taking 'cuttings' from older, fully-grown plants.

Geraniums are the easiest to grow in this way. Using a sharp knife cut a newly-grown side shoot from the main stem of the plant at the place where they join (**c**). Remove the leaves from the lower half (**d**) and push the shoot deeply into some potting compost (**e**).

Making things grow indoors

'Green hair'
You need:
earthenware flowerpot, dish, coloured crayons, grass seed, bulb fibre or soil.

1 Turn the flowerpot upside down and draw a face on one side with the crayons.

2 Place the flowerpot in the dish. Soak some bulb fibre in water and squeeze the excess water out between your hands. Put a thin layer on the top of the pot and cover it with grass seeds, pressing them gently in place. Keep the dish filled with water.

The water will soak up through the porous pot, and the grass will grow longer and longer on top of the 'head'. Don't forget to give it a haircut sometimes!

Potato plants
You need:
potato, 4 toothpicks or cocktail sticks, jamjar, flower-pots, potting compost, knife.

1 Push four toothpicks into a potato so that they form a cross in the middle. Fill a jamjar with water and place the lower half of the potato, supported on the jar by the sticks, in the water.

2 Keep the jar filled with water and after a week or so roots and shoots will grow from the 'eyes'.

3 When the shoots have grown a little, remove the potato from the jar and cut it into pieces, each with its own shoot. Plant each piece in a pot, well covered with compost. Keep the compost moist and soon you will have a fully-fledged potato plant.

Opposite: a selection of house plants that are both colourful and easy to look after.

C

Looking after house plants

Individually potted house plants are the most common form of indoor plants. Some can be grown from seeds or cuttings, but it is better to buy the young plants, already potted, from gardening and chain stores.

Among the easiest to keep are: Hedera (Ivy), Cissus, Rhoicissus, Ficus (Rubber Plants **a**), Sansevieria (Mother-in-Law's Tongue **e**), Chlorophytum, Tradescantia (**b**), Monstera (Swiss Cheese Plant **c**), Fatsia, Geranium, Impatiens (Busy Lizzy **d**) and Coleus.

Most of these come from the Tropics, so it is important that you keep them in a room where the temperature remains warm and even. (The kitchen, for example, is a bad place to keep plants because of temperature variations and the cooking fumes.)

Keep the plants on the window sill, but do not place them in direct sunlight. Water them about twice a week

a   b   c   d   e

in spring and summer when they are growing vigorously, but only occasionally in the winter months when they are almost dormant.

House plants do not get washed by the rain, which keeps the leaf pores of outdoor plants clear so that they can 'breathe'. It is important, therefore, to dust and sponge the leaves clean from time to time.

When the plants have grown too large for their pots, you should transplant them to larger pots, as described on page 30.

Many of the plants in the list are 'climbers'. In their natural state they grow up towards the sun by attaching themselves round other plants and using them as ladders. You can build a lattice framework for your climbers to grow up using split canes tied together with cotton or wire.

Miniature garden

You need:
large baking tray, potting compost, seedlings, pebbles, charcoal.

1 When the spring comes, grow some seedlings from cherry stones, acorns, orange, lemon and grapefruit pips, or any other seeds you can find. Instructions are on pages 27–29.

2 When the seedlings have grown, place a layer of pebbles and some pieces of charcoal in the bottom of the tray. This will act as a water reservoir to keep the soil from becoming too soggy. Fill the rest of the tray almost to the top with potting compost.

3 You can now begin to plant your miniature garden. Transplant the largest seedlings from the pots to the tray (as shown on page 30) so that they form a row along one side.

4 The smaller seedlings can be planted in the rest of the tray, but allow room in between each plant for the roots to grow.

5 You can even plant small twigs of ash, box, apple and so on which will grow to look like miniature trees. If you want to grow flowers, buy some seeds of small Alpine plants or miniature roses.

6 Sow grass seed in the spaces between the plants.

To make your miniature garden look realistic you could easily make some of the following 'extras'.

a *paths :* these can be made from gravel or sand laid neatly on the grass (when it has begun to grow) in narrow lines.

b *ponds :* use small mirrors with a border of gravel, or even dishes pushed into the soil and filled with water.

c *arches :* you can make an arch from narrow strips of balsa wood. Draw a full-size plan of the arch on a piece of paper. Use a sharp knife to cut the balsa wood into the same lengths as on the plan. Glue the pieces together.

d *fences :* just push a row of matchsticks into the soil, 'head-first', and join them all together with a length of cotton.

Place the tray on a table near the window, with the larger plants along the back. Water the miniature garden just enough to keep the surface always moist.

a

b

c

d

Miniature prairie

You need:

large baking tray, potting compost, white card, cacti, sand, paints, scissors.

1 Mix together equal quantities of potting compost and sand until you have enough almost to fill the tray.

2 Buy a selection of small, inexpensive cacti from a garden supplier. Transplant them from their pots into the mixture of compost and sand. Read page 30 to find out how to do this.

3 Sprinkle a thin layer of sand in between the cacti to cover the surface completely.

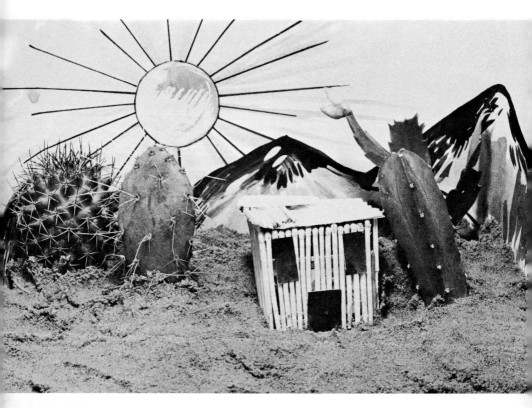

4 Cut a rectangle of card, long enough to wrap around three sides of the tray and about 15 cm. (6 inches) wide. Paint a desert landscape right across it, with mountains, the sun, and other cacti in the distance.

5 Push the lower edge of the card into the earth along the sides of the tray. You could also add a few small rocks, or even a cabin made from matches or drinking straws to add to the desert scene.

Keep the prairie in the warmest room of the house, and in a place where it will get plenty of sun. You only need to water the cacti occasionally because they come from dry, hot desert regions and are able to store water for a long time in their fat stems.

Underwater garden

Not all plants grow on dry land. The sea, ponds, rivers and lakes all contain many types of plants specially adapted for life in the water. Some float freely on the surface, drawing food from the water and drifting with the current. Others are rooted in sand and mud beds and grow towards the surface to get light for 'photosynthesis'.

With these plants you can grow an underwater garden, using an aquarium or even a large glass dish or jar.

You need:
glass aquarium or large jar, potting compost, sand, pencil, water plants from a pet shop.

1 Cover the bottom of the aquarium with a layer of sand about $2\frac{1}{2}$ cm. (1 in.) deep. Cover the sand with a layer of potting compost about the same thickness, and then, on top of this, add another thin layer of sand.

2 Fill the aquarium with water from a jug. Take special care not to disturb the sand when you pour water onto it. Allow the sand plenty of time to settle.

3 Use a pencil to make small holes down into the sand at the bottom of the aquarium. Push the roots of the plants into the holes and carefully press the soil and sand back round the base of the plants.

You can buy water plants in any pet shop that stocks aquaria or you can collect your own plants from ponds and streams. Eel grass, water hyacinth, salvinia, arrowhead, aponogeton, Canadian pondweed, water crowsfoot and duckweed are all suitable for an underwater garden.

Bottle garden

You need:

a large glass jar (with a wide neck), hand drill, potting compost, pebbles, moss, ferns, lichens, tree seedlings, (gathered from the nearest woodland), violet or African violet plant.

1 Remove the lid of the jar and put it to one side.

2 Lay the jar on its side and cover the bottom with a layer of pebbles. Place a layer of potting compost on top of the pebbles.

3 Starting from the far end of the jar and working towards the neck, plant the various seedlings and plants. The violet will add colour to the bottle garden but it does not matter if you do not have one.

4 Press the soil down firmly around the plants and cover the spaces in between with a layer of moss (if you are unable to find any moss, use grass seed instead).

5 Drill a few air holes in the lid of the jar. Moisten the soil by pouring a little water into the jar—this will spread through the pebbles to the far end—and replace the lid.

Put the jar in a light place but not in direct sunlight. Keep the soil moist. Water will collect on the glass inside the jar and run back down into the soil again so you will not have to water the bottle garden very often.

Making things grow out of doors

Window-boxes
You need:
softwood 15 × 2 cm. (6 × ¾ in.) and three times the length of your windowsill, oval wire nails 4 cm. (1½ in.) long, hammer, tenon saw, ruler, pencil, oil-based paint, hand drill.

1 Measure the length of your windowsill and check that it is at least 15 cm. (6 in.) wide.

2 Saw off three equal lengths of wood, each one 13 cm. (5 in.) shorter than the length of the windowsill. Then saw off two pieces 19 cm. (7½ in.) long for the ends of the box.

3 Drill several large drainage holes in one of the long pieces of wood, forming the bottom of the box.

4 Nail the other two long pieces of wood along the sides of the bottom piece so that they form a 'U' shape. Nail the two smaller pieces across the ends to form a trough.

5 Paint the box all over, inside and out, with two coats of a dull-coloured paint.

When the paint has dried, put a layer of broken clay pot or pebbles in the bottom of the box, and place the box on the windowsill, supported by two small blocks of wood. Fill the box with soil or potting compost. You can plant bulbs or seedlings in the box just as you can in a garden.

Preparing the ground

If you are fortunate enough to live in a house with a garden, ask your parents to let you have a small area in which to grow your own plants.

Unless the ground has already been prepared for planting, you must first remove all the weeds which would otherwise prevent the plants from growing. Many weeds have underground stems called 'rhizomes', and you should try to pull out as many as possible by hand.

The best time to dig the garden is when the soil is fairly moist and crumbly. Make sure that you dig to the full depth of the spade or fork. Turn the soil over, break up the large lumps with the spade, and remove the rest of the weeds as you come across them.

When you have finished digging, rake the surface of the soil to make it fine and level. If you rake from one side of the patch to the other, you will find that all the large stones will collect along one edge and these can be used to make an attractive border.

Gardens are best dug twice a year; once in the autumn, to remove dead plants and loosen the soil before winter frosts, and again in the spring to prepare the ground for planting.

Now you are ready to plant out seedlings and young plants in your garden. You could even arrange them in a design like the large butterfly on the facing page. On page 54 you can read how to do it.

Above: all the tools you need for your own patch of garden—forks, watering can, rake, spade and hoe.

Opposite: hanging gardens (page 60) and window-boxes (page 48) combine to make a very gay balcony.

Weed garden

The easiest plants to grow are weeds which flourish without any human help. Mark off an area of your garden with a border of stones and leave it undisturbed. You will be amazed at the number and variety of weeds that will soon appear. See how many you can identify.

Flower garden

The most popular type of garden is one that contains a variety of colourful flowers. It is important, if you want your display to be impressive, to plan the position of all the different plants in advance.

First draw a plan of your garden patch on a sheet of graph paper. Shade areas with coloured pencils to help you decide where to put the different types of plant. Use the squares to help you plan designs like the butterfly on page 51. Arrange the plants according to size, with the larger varieties at the back (possibly against a wall) and the small border plants along the front edge. You can even arrange the seeds of the border plants to spell out your name when they grow.

Most garden flowers can be raised from seeds. They can be grown first indoors in seed trays and the seedlings can be transplanted to the garden in the early summer as described on page 30. If you plant the seeds directly in the garden you must wait until the weather is warmer otherwise the seedlings may die.

On page 66 there is a list of plants that are suitable for your patch of garden. Choose varieties that bloom at different times of the year so that your garden is always in flower.

Here is a plan of a small garden patch and a drawing of the well-balanced garden it grew into with a climbing rose and taller plants against the wall at the back.

If you want your plants to grow in neat rows, especially where they form a border display, push two sticks into the ground at the ends of the row and tie a piece of string tightly between them (see facing page). Make a shallow groove along this line with a pencil and sprinkle the seeds evenly along its length. Cover the seeds with a thin layer of soil. Remove the string, but leave the sticks where they are. Push the empty seed packet onto one of the sticks to help you identify the seedlings when they grow.

Seedlings should be replanted fairly close together in the garden, not only because the display will look more beautiful, but also because the weeds will have greater difficulty in finding somewhere to grow. Any weeds that do grow can easily be removed by carefully hoeing between the plants. Use a short, slicing movement with the blade of the hoe just below the surface of the ground (see facing page). You should keep the soil moist by watering it thoroughly.

Your plants may be one of three kinds:
a annuals: these flower for one year only.
b biennials: these last for two years. They produce only leaves and roots in the first year and flowers the next year.
c perennials: plants that last for three or more years, flowering every year.
Each autumn you should remove the dead annuals. Leave the others undisturbed. When the perennials begin to take up a lot of room you can dig them up in the spring, split them into smaller clumps, and replant them.

Kitchen garden

Many of the vegetables and herbs that you see in super-markets can easily be grown from seed in your patch of garden. Follow the instructions on pages 27–28.

Here are some ideas for making vegetable-growing more fun:

a marrows (in Britain) or squashes (in America): If your friends can be persuaded to grow them too, you could hold a 'biggest marrow' or 'biggest squash' contest. Start the seeds off in pots and transplant them. Feed the soil well by digging in plenty of compost before you plant the seeds or seedlings. Pages 62–63 tell you how to make a compost heap.

b beans: Climbing varieties need long, bamboo sticks around which they can wind as they grow. If you plant a row of them you can hold a 'bean Olympics' to see which one wins the race to the top.

c potatoes: How many potatoes can be grown from one? For the best results, use seed potatoes planted in holes about 30 cm. (1 ft.) apart. When shoots appear above the surface, use a trowel to build up the earth in ridges around the stems so that more potatoes have room to form. When the stalks of the plants go yellow, the new potatoes will have formed underground. Lift each plant with a fork and see how many potatoes have grown around the roots.

Other vegetables that are easy to grow are: broccoli, onions, cabbage, Brussels sprouts, carrots, lettuce, peas, tomatoes and cucumbers. In each case follow the instructions on the seed packets.

Keep one section of your kitchen garden for herbs such as parsley, thyme, chives, sage, basil, rosemary, tarragon, marjoram and fennel. Grow them in clumps so that they are easily picked and make sure you label them clearly. If you want to grow mint, plant it in an old bucket with holes in the bottom. This will stop the roots from spreading too far.

59

Hanging garden

You need:

old lampshade frame, wire netting, potting compost, large screw hook, strong string, sphagnum moss (from a flower shop), pliers.

1 Cut the wire netting with the pliers so that it fits inside the lampshade frame, covering the narrow end. You need not cut an exact shape because the wire can easily be bent, and it does not matter if it overlaps in places.

2 Place a layer of sphagnum moss on the wire netting to form a dish-shaped lining in the frame. Fill the frame with potting compost.

3 Put the seedlings of trailing plants into the potting compost and water them in well. You could use variegated ivy, trailing lobelia, tradescantia, petunias, campanula isophylla and others.

4 Tie three equal lengths of string together at one end and tie the other ends to the top of the basket so that it will hang level.

5 Screw the hook into a wooden arch or porch so that the basket will hang freely.

As the plants grow, they will trail over the sides of the basket, producing a colourful cascade. You could hang the lampshade inside an old sunhat or basket to make it even more colourful like those on page 52.

Hints for outdoor gardens

Improving the soil
To get the best from your garden, you must take as much care of your soil as you do of your plants.

Not all soils are alike in quality. Loam is the ideal, containing a perfect mixture of sand, clay, chalk and humus. You may, however, find that your patch has too much of one of these and not enough of the others. Chalky and sandy soils dry out very quickly, losing their minerals at the same time. To enable this type of soil to hold water better, and to replace the minerals that have been washed away, you should dig in plenty of compost. Soils with too much clay become water-logged in wet weather and crack open when it is very dry. Drainage can be improved by digging in lime and sieved ashes from a fire.

All types of soil can be improved by adding humus (which consists of dead and decayed animal and plant matter) to lighten the soil and provide more food for growing plants. You can collect humus in the woods or buy it from gardening shops.

Making a compost heap
Pile all the dead plants, weeds and grass cuttings from your garden, together with vegetable waste from the kitchen neatly in one corner of the garden. Bacteria will slowly turn this waste material into valuable compost. Build up the compost heap in layers, and always take compost from the bottom of the pile for digging into the soil. Cover the heap with sacking. 'Composting' can be speeded up by adding a thin sprinkling of chalk between the layers or by using an 'activator' from a gardening shop.

Using fertilizers

As plants grow, they use up the mineral salts of the soil. If you grew the same plants year after year without replacing these salts, the soil would slowly become barren. Nitrogen, phosphates and potash are the most important of these minerals, and they can be added to the soil by using a 'compound' fertilizer bought from a gardening shop.

Getting rid of pests and diseases

Many small creatures, such as greenfly and red spider mite, live by feeding on both indoor and outdoor plants.

It is important to give your plants a careful inspection every so often, especially the undersides of the leaves, to make sure these pests have not gathered there. If they do appear in large numbers, spray or powder the leaves with insecticides from a garden supplier. Follow the instructions very carefully because some of the insecticides can be harmful to human beings and pets.

Many pests that live in the soil, such as slugs and snails, may also harm your plants. They may either eat the roots or crawl up the stems and eat the leaves. Again, garden suppliers will advise you as to which insecticide will be most suitable, but you can help by killing any of these pests that you come across while digging and weeding.

Birds may be just as destructive in your garden as insects, especially at seed-planting time. They will scratch below the thin covering of soil and eat the seeds before they have a chance to grow. You can prevent this from happening by placing short sticks all around the seed patch and then stringing black cotton between the sticks and over the seed bed, rather like a spider's web. If birds are still attracted to the seed bed, hang strips of tinfoil from the cotton. The wind will blow the strips about, and the movement and noise will frighten birds away. You could even build a proper scarecrow from old clothes, newspapers and sticks.

Flowers to grow from seeds

Flower	Colour(s)	Type	When to plant
Ageratum	blue	annual	March
Alyssum	white	annual	spring
Antirrhinum (Snapdragon)	various	annual	early spring*
Aster	various	annual	spring
Aubretia	pinks/mauves	perennial	May/June
Canterbury bell	blue	biennial	spring
Carnation	various	perennial	February*
Chrysanthe-mum	various	perennial	February*
Clarkia	various	annual	spring
Cornflower	blue	annual	spring
Dahlia	various	perennial	spring
Daisy	various	perennial	late spring
Delphinium	blue/white	perennial	summer
Digitalis	various	biennial	late spring
Geranium (Pelargonium)	various	perennial	January*
Geum	orange/red	perennial	summer
Globe Amaranth (Batchelor's button)	various	annual	spring
Godetia	reds	annual	spring
Gypsophila	white	ann./peren.	spring
Hollyhock	various	biennial	summer
Larkspur	various	annual	spring
Lobelia	blue/white	annual	spring
Lupin	various	perennial	late spring
Marigold	orange/yellow	annual	late spring
Myosotis	blue	biennial	late spring
Nasturtium	orange/yellow	annual	late spring
Nemesia	various	annual	spring*
Nigella (Love-in-a-mist)	various	annual	spring

Flower	Colour(s)	Type	When to plant
Pansy	various	biennial	spring
Petunia	various	annual	spring
Phlox	various	annual	March*
Pinks (Dianthus)	various	perennial	April*
Polyanthus	various	perennial	Jan./Feb.*
Poppy	various	annual	spring
Salvia	red	annual	early spring*
Scabious	mauve	annual	spring
Stock	various	annual	spring
Sunflower (Helianthus)	various	annual	spring
Sweet pea	various	annual	spring
Sweet William	various	biennial	late spring
Wallflower	orange/yellow	biennial	early summer
Zinnia	various	annual	spring

* these flowers are best grown as indoor seedlings and then transplanted to the garden

Index

1977